THE BOUNCE BACK

THE JOURNEY FROM THE DEEPEST LOW'S TO THE HIGHEST UP'S

M. HARSHA VARDHAN

Copyright © M. Harsha Vardhan
All Rights Reserved.

This book has been published with all efforts taken to make the material error-free after the consent of the author. However, the author and the publisher do not assume and hereby disclaim any liability to any party for any loss, damage, or disruption caused by errors or omissions, whether such errors or omissions result from negligence, accident, or any other cause.

While every effort has been made to avoid any mistake or omission, this publication is being sold on the condition and understanding that neither the author nor the publishers or printers would be liable in any manner to any person by reason of any mistake or omission in this publication or for any action taken or omitted to be taken or advice rendered or accepted on the basis of this work. For any defect in printing or binding the publishers will be liable only to replace the defective copy by another copy of this work then available.

Dedicated

*To my family and friends who always
believed that i can achieve something.
To all those mad cricket lovers who are
never tired of watching test cricket...*

Contents

Foreword

The records will mention that India won the Border-Gavaskar trophy in 2021, but it never tells the story which is much more than the victory. And this wonderful story is perfectly narrated by the author of The Bounce Back.

The Bounce Back is the finest way to retrieve the glorious moments of India's triumph at the Gabba fortress. This read is an analysis of the nations historic test series and also an embodiment of a life lesson. The Bounce back showed the courage and character of every detail in the play.

The breach of the Gabba fortress is an iconic moment which is close to the hearts of every Indian cricket lover and the soul of it is captured in this read. This victory is a revolutionary win and The Bounce Back is the perfect celebration for it. This is the most irresistible page-turner for every reader and is a must-read.

Preface

The Bounce Back - it's the journey of the Indian team through their high's and low's during the 2020-21 Test series against Australia for the Border Gavaskar Trophy. History has been created winning the series and i in this book will make sure you ; the reader to relive those moments, to relive one of the wrost nightmare and some of the wildest dreams coming true that we never imagined.

This book isn't just what you have seen during the match or series, this book contained the emotions and feelings that every indian went through during the series. History has been created and now it's time we see and know what really made the history to be created and how proud the Indian team can be of themselves.

This work is a tribute to that Indian team who fought back hard when they had a chance to rot and die. This is my first book as an author and certainly hope that you feel the same way how i felt and writing it...

Acknowledgements

They say that writing is a lonely profession. They lie. An outstanding group of people have come together to make this book possible. And I would like to thank them.

Kasyap is one of my friends who edited the cover page and also helped me in writing the book. Thanmai for making sure I am always on the right track while at work.

When I was done with my script and waiting for publishers, one of my friends, Leela Krishna, showed me a way on how to publish this book for me, and today I can say that it's only his advice that made it possible to publish this book.

Parveen had a helping hand in completing this book. My friends always showed faith in me and stood by me in writing this.

When I was done with the script and thinking about how this book would be, the foreword written by Sreeja Veeramreddy Garu gave me the confidence that I did better than what I expected.

Also, my special thanks to the CRIC BUZZ app developers. The scores all over this book are drawn from it and provide a lot of information about the series on how the pitches are and where the matches are held.

And finally a special thanks to the #22 batch who supported me throughout the rough patch that i went by and believed

ACKNOWLEDGEMENTS

that i can overcome it and make something that would make me happy.

Prologue

"This is going to be it " said my father as we both were watching the match on the TV. India needs 3 more runs to win the series and to create history.

In the next ball, pant hit the boundary winning the match for India. Me and my father are shouting and cheering as the Indian team is celebrating the win. We both hugged and patted each other's shoulders. Unknowingly tears started to roll down my cheeks. The tears of joy and happiness.

And when I look back at what happened throughout the series, I felt like I was climbing Mount Everest without any gear or experience, just with the courage in the heart and the rage in the eyes. A thought struck me of how I would be writing a book on the series and the book you see now is the outcome of that.

CHAPTER ONE

The Beginning

19/01/2021,Brisbane.

It's 5:30 in the evening at the Gabba stadium. The last day of the final test match between Australia and India is coming to an end. The supporters in the stadium are on their feet, cheering their respective teams. India requires 3 runs to win the test match, series and to create history by winning back-to-back test series on Australian soil.

India's new batting sensation, Rishabh Pant, is on strike and Hazelwood is going to bowl the ball. Pant plays a low full toss outside off stump near to the 4th stump and Pant sends it along the ground to long off. Pant is running hard to win the match only when he realises that the fielder is not placed at long off and the ball is travelling towards the boundary.

As the winning runs were hit, there was a large roar from the crowd. All the cricket admirers know that this series is going to be one of the best ever played. Cricket lovers know how hard it's been for the Indian team to achieve this.

As I was watching the Indian team celebrations, tears started to roll down my cheeks. My heart became heavy with feelings. I went back to the time when the series started. I could see how each day of the matches went by as the time progressed.

Great comebacks are those that come after the greatest failures. This is such a great comeback that came from the Indian team in the Aus. vs Ind Test series in 2020-21. The people of India have high hopes for the Indian team after they won the Border-Gavaskar trophy in 2018-19 by defeating Australia in the first test series in Indian cricket history.

However, many said that the reason behind India's winning the test series in 2018-19 is the absence of Australia's best batsmen, Steve Smith and David Warner, who are banned from playing cricket for one year because of the ball tampering that happened in a test series against South Africa in 2018.

But what actually mattered is that it's not just the absence of Smith and Warner that made India win the series but also the Indian players' stepping up at the right time when needed for the team that helped India seal the 4 match test series with a 2-1.

Virat Kohli became the first Indian and Asian captain to win a Test series on Australian soil against Australia. It's been a dream test series for the Indian middle order wall, Cheteshwar Pujara, scoring a whopping total of 521 runs from 1258 balls, also being the highest run getter in the series.

It's been nearly two years since the historic test series win and India are once again touring Australia for a 3 match ODI, 3 match T20 and 4 match Test series.

The Australian team won the three-match ODI series 2-1, while the Indian team came back strongly to win the T20 series 2-1.With both the ODI and T20 series being won by each of the teams, the focus has now shifted towards the test series.

What made the test series even more special was the presence of their batsmen, Steve Smith, David Warner, and Australia's new batting sensation, Marcus Labuschagne, in their side. While India is expecting their test specialist, Pujara, to continue his form from the last series in 2018-19,

The Indians are hoping to see a great batting display from their captain, Virat Kohli, as he is playing his one and only test and going back to India for personal reasons.

CHAPTER TWO

The Setback

15/12/2020, Adelaide

For every story, there has to be a start, and there is also a start for the story I am writing. A start which will be remembered as one of the worst of all time in Test cricket history and Indian cricket history. A start that no Indian could have imagined, and one that no one would want to be in.

It started well for India on the 1st day of the 1st test match as the Indian Captain, Virat Kohli, won the toss and decided to bat first. Virat has a record of not losing matches in Test cricket when he wins the toss. Destiny, on the other hand, has other plans for him and his men.

After the first innings, India had a total of 244 all out, with Pujara, Virat Kohli, and Rahane scoring the majority of the runs, while all other batters failed to score. When the Australians batted in their first innings, Indian bowlers bowled extremely well, limiting them to 191 runs, giving India a 53-run lead from their first innings.

The lead of 53 made India a strong side to win the test. The Indians are hoping to bat well in the second innings and get most of the runs and are thinking of keeping the Australians under present. But destiny had other plans for the Indian side.

When the Indian side started to bat in their 2nd innings, it took no time for the Indians to realise that they were on the losing side in the match. The ball that touched the bat of an Indian is going directly to the hands of fielders. The Australian pacer, Josh Hazelwood, bowled really beautifully to pick up his first wicket in the 2nd innings.

With the display of some good bowling from the Australians and a poor batting display from the Indian batters, India was 36/9 all out, which is the lowest innings score for an Indian team in the history of Indian cricket. No Indian batsmen scored in double figures. Australia easily chased the target of 89 and made a good start to the series with a lead of 1-0 in the 4-match series.

The Indian team at Adelaide went down like a setting sun. Many trolled and laughed at the Indian team, much like the darkness laughed at the setting sun. Many believed that there was no way that an Indian team could rise and win the series.

With their best batsman, Virat Kohli, returning home and the defeat in the first match, the Indian team is completely down in the series and in morale.

With Rahane as captain for the remaining series, the Indian team knew that the only way to forget their defeat was to fight back hard. The Indian team desired to rise like the early morning sun, which replaces darkness with light.

They knew they had to fight back the right way. But how well do you think they will fight back? How good are they at forgetting the defeat and rising again? Only time knows. Who are we to judge a team with only one match?

CHAPTER THREE

The Come Back

26/12/2020, MCG, Melbourne

Welcome back to the 2nd test match of the 4-match series between India and Australia. On one side Australia came into the match with high confidence after their first win against India. They are surely favourites after the way how their bowlers bowled at the Adelaide. They wanted to keep the momentum and win the 2nd test so as to have a higher advantage for winning the series.

India on the other side with their best batsman away in home and from the defeat of their 1st match are lower side. Rahane became the captain for the remaining series. India is hoping to fight back hard show what they are after their worst ever defeat in the first match.

It's Australia who won the toss and decided to bat. Australians are playing with no change while India have made a few changes to their side. There are two debutants for India Shubman Gill and Mohammad Siraj and are playing with Rishabh pant and Jadeja on their side.

Australia is 195 all-out in their first innings. It has been a great bowling display from Indian bowlers. Bumrah and Ashwin had completely out played the Australian batsmen by taking 7 wickets in total. The debutant Siraj impressed everyone by taking 2 wickets while Jadeja having one wicket to his name.

India however couldn't be able to get a good start as like from their 1st test. They lost Agarwal very early in the last ball of the 1st over. Gill played an impressive knock of 45 and had a good stand with Pujara. These both batsmen when are setting got out by Cummins in 10 balls. Now all is upon the shoulders of their captain Rahane.

Rahane and Vihari had a good partnership which really kept India in the game. They played defensively for a period of time and stopped the flow of wickets. A good start Vihari was out by Lyon. However, on the other end Rahane kept going getting those crucial runs and kept the game in the Indian side. Pant played good but not enough for the side. He played his natural game and had a good partnership with Rahane. When pant was Jadeja came to bat with the Indian captain.

Jadeja is the last hope for Indian team. They know that the partnership between Rahane and Jadeja has to be crucial for the team. Rahane and Jadeja played really well and kept the score board ticking. They made India go past the Indian score and took India to lead. Meanwhile Rahane got his 50 from 111 balls.

The partnership between Rahane and Jadeja kept India on the upper side of the match. They both played fabulously to took the lead to 70 in the mean while Rahane scored his 12th international century,2nd against Australia and 2nd at the MCG . This century from the captain showed the character he possessed in the match.

Rahane after his century was runout and Jadeja scored a well-made 50.However the last 5 wickets were fallen for just 32 runs. India finally finished their total with 326 with a lead of 131 runs. India expected a lead of above 150 or above when their captain and all-round Jadeja were Playing well. However, all the hopes were lost when the partnership was broken and wickets went down quickly.

When Australia came to bat in the second innings it's again the Indian bowlers that bowled excellent lengths and made the Australian's face the problems. The debutant Siraj took a 3-wicket haul and Bumrah ,Ashwin and Jadeja had 2 wickets each and the Umesh has one wicket to his name.

The Australian young all-rounder Green played a good innings scoring 45 from 146 balls. Green and Cummins has a good partnership which however failed to score runs but stopped the wickets flow for a good Australia finished their innings at 200 all-out.

India needs a total of 72 runs to win the test match also level the series. Draw is no more an option as there are two days of play left. Gill and Agarwal opened the Indian 2nd innings. India lost two quick wickets of both Agarwal and Pujara. The Indian Captain and the Young debutant led India to the victory.

This victory will always be remembered as one the best in the history of Indian cricket. A team that is 36 all-out in their last test, a team which had their best batsman away from they them and a team with their new captain leading them. Many might had thought that Indian team was out of the series when they were 36 all-out at Adelaide. But none made them give up their fighting. They fought back hard with a roared like a lion and levelled the series.

A come back from the worst set back is always special. A come back that will always be remembered as on the best forever. The ghosts of Adelaide have been buried by a memorable win at Melbourne.

CHAPTER FOUR

The Unbowed Character

07/01/2021,Sydney,

Welcome to the 3rd test of the 4-match test series between India and Australia. The series is equally level, with each team winning the first 2 tests. India, having won the last test from the ghosts of the first test, are high on confidence. The way the Indian team fought back after the first team will always be remembered by every Indian cricket fan all over the world.

On the other hand, Australia, having won the 1st test, has lost their momentum in the 2nd test. Their batting hasn't been good in their last two tests. So, they are looking forward to displaying some great batting.

India is losing their experienced players in the form of injuries. Shami, who got injured in the first test, has been out of the whole series and another experienced pacer, Umesh, who was injured in the second test, has also been out of the series. After an injury recovery Rohit Sharma is coming into the team and Saini is making his debut for India in tests. The young Australian batsman, Will Pucovski, is also making his debut.

It was Australia who won the toss and decided to bat first. India had an early break through but was unable to capitalise on the opportunity. Will Pucovski, a debutant, and young man Labuschagne toiled against the Indian bowlers, putting on a 100-run partnership. Pucovski made his first half century on his debut and was out for 62 by the other debutant, Saini. Labuschagne and Steve Smith, on the other hand, had another brilliant 100-run partnership. Australia was 200-2 and were in total control of the game.

Then something special happened. The Indian team have done something that they have been doing since their first test. They fought back hard after dismissing Labuschagne. Smith, on the other hand, batted brilliantly but is lacking partners. Australia was confined to 338 all out of 200-2. However, it's Steve Smith's batting that is the highlight of the innings. He made a brilliant 131 runs from 216 balls.

When India batted in the first innings, both openers, Rohit and Gill, played well to help India reach 50 without losing a wicket. Hazelwood provided the hosts with a breakthrough in the form of Rohit just as they appeared to be set. After Rohit's dismissal, Gill went on to bring up his first fifty in his career. He was immediately out after reaching his milestone. Rahane and Pujara played some good innings to stop the flow of wickets. However, after Rahane's dismissal, there has been a flow of wickets. Pujara, on the other hand, showed some resilience and batted really well to bring up his fifty from 176 balls and was immediately out after his 50. Jadeja and Pant made some good runs for their team, but not enough.

India ended their first innings at 244 all-out. Australia had a lead of 94 runs in their first innings.

When Australia came back to bat in their second innings, they lost both their openers very quickly. And it was once again Labuschagne and Steve Smith who shared a 103-run partnership. Labuschagne was dismissed at 73 by Saini and Wade went out without troubling the scoreboard. Then Steve

Smith and Australian captain Tim Paine had a partnership of 60 runs between them. Smith was dismissed at 81 by Ashwin, which brought the Young Australian Green into the play. Green played an excellent knock for 84 runs from 132 balls and was out by Bumrah.

As soon as Green was dismissed, Tim Paine declared the Australian innings as soon as Green was dismissed. There was a lot on the ground when India bowled Australia's second innings. Some members of the Australian crowd racially abused the young player, Siraj, and the game was temporarily halted. Also, after the end of the 3rd day of the test, some of the spectators racially abused the Indian bowler, Bumrah. The Indian team complained about it to the Australian cricket board.

When India came to bat in the second innings, they needed a mammoth total of 407 runs to win the test. The Indian openers provided a good opening partnership and had 71 runs in between them. Gill went out in the form of the first wicket for India by Hazelwood and Rohit after his fifty was out by Cummins. The Indian captains, Rahane and Pujara, made sure that they did not lose the wickets on the remaining day. The Indians ended their day at 98-2.

India needed 309 runs to win the test on the last day of the match, while Australia needed 8 more wickets to win the match and go up in the series. The day started well for Australia as their spinner, Lyon, dismissed Rahane in the very 2nd over of the day. To everyone's surprise, the young wicket keeper batsman, Rishabh Pant, has been promoted up the order and came to bat after Rahane was dismissed.

Pant, who is naturally an attacking player, played his own style of game. On the other hand, Pujara is doing what he always does. Pant is going after the bowlers, particularly their spinner Lyon, and making him pay for his actions. The pair batted brilliantly and made sure that they didn't lose another wicket before lunch. In the meantime, Pant reached 50 and continued to attack the bowlers when necessary, putting pressure on them. Pujara, on the other hand, played his own natural game of defending the balls and helped pace by rotating the strike.

The pair put on an impressive 104 runs in between them before lunch. India needed 201 runs to win the match and batted in the last two sessions to win the match. All knew that the result of the match would depend upon how long the Pujara and Pant pair stayed in the middle. Pujara, after lunch, brought up his 6000-run milestone in test cricket from 134 innings. He also brought up his second fifty in the match from 170 balls.

When both the batsmen are set and taking India to victory, things change dramatically. Pant was dismissed by Lyon on 97 when he was looking on for a shot to bring up his century. Such was his innings. No one has the right to say anything about his aggression. The aggression which Pant showed is what made India believe in Winning the test and the aggression were what kept hopes alive for many. The aggressive nature of the pants led us to believe that the Indian team was fighting to win the match rather than to draw the best. The pant knock gave the team and Indians all over the world a lot of confidence. The Pant Knock of 97 will always be remembered as one of the best from him.

Pant and Pujara combined for 148 runs, the highest partnership for India in the fourth innings. After

Pant's dismissal, Pujara took on the bowlers and looked in solid touch. But Pujara was dismissed by Hazelwood. There it is for India to be in the commanding position on the back foot. Both of their set batsmen were sent back to the pavilion. The rest of the batsmen were either injured or tail-enders and India had no hope of winning or drawing the test.

Ashwin, who has been suffering from back pain, has come to bat ahead of Jadeja . Vihari, on the other hand, is limping. They had 45+ overs to defend with just 5 wickets in hand, and for every Indian, it's a hopeless situation. The Vihari-Ashwin pair knew that winning was no longer an option because of the injuries they were having. But defending 45+ overs against a top-class bowling unit is something even tougher.

The pair started defending the balls that were thrown at them. Ashwin took blows on his hand, chest, and waist, but he was immovable. Vihari, on the other hand, even with his hamstring, kept on defending the balls. They batted, batted and batted like they were the last to stop India's fall and keep everyone alive. The pain of their injuries kept on increasing, but the pain was nothing in comparison to their determination.

With each passing year, the hopes of Indians rise. The pair have been bullied and sledged, but they kept their temptation to themselves because, right now, nothing is more important to them than saving the test for India. "I am excited for the Gabba test," are the words from Tim Paine that sledged Ashwin while they were playing. The pair played 259 balls in between them with a partnership of 40+ runs. They made sure that the day ended with no more wickets lost for India and also that neither of the two were out by the day's end.

It's been called The Great Escape for the Indian team, but in truth, it's not an escape, it's the character that the Indian players showed that made them not lose the match. With the pain they were in, the Vihari-Ashwin duo had the option of retiring and going out to the pavilion, but neither did because they saw nothing more important to them than saving the test for India, and they had done it.

India batted 131 overs in the fourth innings of the test, which is their highest since 1980. The fighting spirit that the Indian team showed when nothing went their way showed how determined they were and their unbowed character showed how dangerous a team can be.

CHAPTER FIVE

The Final Test

Brisbane, 15 January 2021

All was set for the last test of the 4-match series between India and Australia. The Indian team, on the other hand, is confident after their performance in the previous test and is hoping to have a good game here at the Gabba. The major concern that the Indian team has is the injuries their players are suffering. The Indian team hardly had their 11 members to pick from. On the other hand, Australia is confident that they can win the match and series because it's the venue that brought them such confidence.

The Gabba has been an unbeatable fortress for Australia for the last 32 years. The Australian team hasn't lost a test match in Gabba since 1989, and with their best 11 line-up, they're hoping to win the match series and reclaim the Border-Gavaskar trophy.

India had two new debutants for the match in the form of T.Natarajan and Washington Sundar and also brought Thakur. The heroes of the 3rd test, Ashwin and Vihari, are not playing the final test because of injuries, and India's main pace bowler, Bumrah, will not be playing the match because of health issues. For Australia, it's their best 11 standing against India's last 11.

It was Australia who won the toss and elected to bat first. Also, the bowling attack of the two teams had a huge difference in terms of their experience and wickets. The bowling attack of Australia had 1000+ wickets to their name, while the Indian bowling attack has just 13 wickets, which includes the 2 wickets of Rohit Sharma.

Early in the innings, the Indian team is able to find the breakthrough by dismissing Warner and Harris. Then it's once again the Labuschagne and Smith pair that started to build a good partnership and had 70 runs in between them, which was finally broken by the debutant Sundar, who had his first wicket in his career.

After Smith's dismissal, Wade and Labuschagne had an excellent partnership. They took the score from 87-3 to 200-3 and it was then the other debutant pacer, T.Natarajan, who took the wicket of Wade and broke the partnership. In the meantime, Labuschagne brought up his 100 and was caught by Natarajan at 108. Both the set batsmen were out, and it was when the Australian captain and Green had a good partnership. They had nearly 100 runs in between them and were looking in good shape.

Sundar then dismissed Green at 47, and Paine was dismissed by Thakur after Paine's fifty. The tailenders of the Australian team made some quick runs and were able to cross the 350 mark. Australia finished their innings at 369.

India started their first innings with a quick wicket fall. Gill was dismissed early in the innings. While Rohit played some good shots and looked in good touch, He is dismissed by Lyon when Rohit is trying for an aggressive shot. Then both Pujara and Rahane made sure that they didn't lose any wickets on the day.

On day 3, Rahane and Pujara started the innings slowly, and Pujara was dismissed by Hazelwood and Rahane was dismissed by Starc. India was unable to establish a good partnership and lost wickets. They were 186-6 at one stage.

Just Everyone thought that Australia was going to have a massive lead, but the young batsmen, Sundar and Thakur, had other plans in their mind. Though they are young and inexperienced, it never showed in their batting.

Both Sundar and Thakur took the Indian team score from 186-6 to cross over 300. In the meantime, Thakur brought up his first fifty in his test career and was later dismissed by Cummins at 67. On the other hand, Sundar also gave good support to Thakur by playing some excellent shots. These two players added 123 runs in between them. After the partnership was broken, India ended their first innings for 336 all-out.

From 186-6 to 336 all out, the innings is all about the courage shown by the two young and inexperienced players, Sundar and Thakur. They not just only reduced the lead for Australia but also showed that the Indian team can never be underestimated until they are over and out.

Australia had a lead of 33 runs from their first innings. In Australia's second innings ,the openers gave them a good start. The openers had a partnership of 89 runs in between them and were broken by Thakur. Then the other opener, Warner, was dismissed after his first wicket by Siraj. In the 1st innings, Labuschagne started attacking the bowlers from the start. The intent of the Australian team is clear: to score as many runs as possible and give a massive total for India to chase.

Labuschagne was dismissed for 25 runs by Siraj, and then Australia lost another wicket immediately after Labuschagne's dismissal in the form of Wade. Then Steve Smith and Green added some crucial runs for the team. In the meantime, Smith brought up his fifty. Smith was dismissed by Siraj with an excellent delivery which had an unexpected bounce in it and it took Smith by Smith and all he could do was just have to have a tip on his bat handle to find Rahane at slip.

After Smith and Green's dismissal, Australia lost wickets every now and then, and then Cummins made some quick runs for his team. But the hero of the innings is the young Indian pacer, Siraj. He took his first five-fifer in his career. The last two months have been very tough for him. He lost his father when he came to Australia for the series, and he didn't even attend his last rituals for his father.

His father's dream to see his son playing for the test team has come true, but he is not there to see it. The courage that he showed during this test series is something that inspires everyone. With just

2 tests' experience, the way he led the Indian pace attack in the last test of the series was astonishing and inspiring.

Australia was 294 all-out in their second innings and they gave a total of 328 for the Indian team to chase down. The 4th day of play when India started their 2nd innings was obstructed by rain and has been suspended for the remainder of the day.

Everything was set for the final day of play of the last test. Australia needed 10 wickets to win the match and win the Border-Gavaskar trophy, and for India, they needed 328 runs to win the match and series, or to play the whole day and draw the match and keep the Border-Gavaskar trophy with them.

CHAPTER SIX

The Breaches of GABBA

At the start of day 5, the game looked evenly poised for both the teams. 324 runs with 10 wickets in hand is not a tough chance, but also not easy with the pitch having cracks and the uneven bounce the pitch is offering makes it even tougher for batsmen to read the ball and play their shots. And the bowling attack that the Australian team had made it even harder for India to play. But a few good partnerships can help India see the day end.

The Indian team knew all the hard work they had been doing for the last 30 days had come to an end. The fighting spirit they displayed following the devastating loss in the first test, as well as the resilience displayed by the Indian team following the first match, their comeback from the ghosts of Adelaide at the MCG and the unbowed character they displayed when all odds were stacked against them at the SCG, have all come to an end. All they have to do is to put up their hands for the one last time in the series and make sure they either win or draw the match.

Early in the day, Cummins gave a shock to the Indian team by dismissing Rohit. The next batsman is Pujara, who comes to bat. He knew he had a massive role to play and ensure his team reached the other end in their favour. Gill and Pujara both played with much focus and showed their determination. On the one hand, Gill scores runs from the bad balls and Pujara plays his own natural way of blocking whatever has been thrown at him. Both Pant and Pujara ensured that they didn't lose any wickets for the remaining time in the session. India went to lunch at 83-1.

India needed 245 runs from the remaining two sessions to win the match, while Australia needed just 9 good balls to take them to victory. With the cracks on the pitch and a required rate of 4 per over, it's always going to be tough to chase down.

After lunch, both Pujara and Gill played some good cricket shots. Mainly, the young Gill took on Starc and hit him for a six and two fours in three consecutive balls. Gill, while nearing his century, was dismissed by Lyon at 91. What an inning this young man has put in. It was only his third test, but the way he batted against top-tier bowlers demonstrated his tenacity. It would have been excellent if he could have reached the three-figure mark, but still, this innings from him is going to be one of the finest and best from him.

After Gill's dismissal, Rahane came to bat. Rahane batted like he and his team were determined to win the tournament. He made some quick runs of 24 from 22 balls and was dismissed by Cummins. Pant came to bat after Rahane's dismissal. Both Pant and Pujara ensured that they didn't lose any wickets for the remaining session. India went to lunch at 183-3. They scored a run in the 2nd session and lost Gill and Rahane.

India needed 145 runs from the remaining 37 overs left to win, while Australia needed 7 wickets to win the match. All four results are possible and could happen. After the tea break, India started their batting slowly and scored just 11 runs from 7 overs. 134 runs are needed from 30 overs. The required rate reached 4.5 per cent. Then Pant smashed a six-against Lyon and four-against Starc. Pujara also started scoring runs when possible. He brought up his fifty by hitting a four against Labuschagne.

This fifty has been the slowest ever off his bat. He has taken 196 balls to bring up his fifty. It's not just the number of balls he faced, but there's a lot more to it. The courage he showed even when he took blows on his helmet and on his shoulders and on his fingers will always be remembered, and his never-give-up attitude to risking his body for the wickets is something that has to be remembered for a long time. Pujara was dismissed by Cummins after his fifty. It is a huge wicket in the context of the game.

Mayank came to bat after Pujara's dismissal. Also, Pant brought up 1000 runs in his test career from just 27 innings, becoming the fastest Indian wicket-keeper to do so. Pant also brought up his 50 after Pujara's dismissal. It's been a wonderful season so far for him. But his 50 wasn't enough to satisfy. There is much more work to be done.

India needed 87 runs from the last 18 remaining overs. Mayank was dismissed early by Cummins. With each wicket gone, the hopes of India are going down. They know only Pant himself can't do much. He needed someone on the other end to help him. By the time Sundar came to bat after Mayank's dismissal, India needed 61 runs from 12 overs with 5 wickets in hand.

Sundar played some excellent shots and held a good partnership with Pant. He scored the well needed runs there by removing the pressure on the pants. 50 runs were needed from 8 overs. It's now been more than enough. But then Sundar took on the world's number one bowler and hit him for a four and a six in consecutive balls.

also started hitting the ball. At a stage when 39 runs were needed from 7 overs, Pant hit two fours in the Lyon's over and a four came in the form of byes. The Indian team were able to extract 15 runs from that over there by bringing the equation down to 24 runs required from 36 balls. In the next over, which was bowled by Hazelwood, both of them were able to score 9 runs. When 10 runs were required from the 25 balls, Sundar was dismissed by Lyon.

Sundar's dismissal reached a tipping point after Thakur took power. Hazelwood's over ended when

Pant then struck a four of the very 1st ball of Hazelwood's over. However, Thakur was dismissed by Hazelwood trying for a big shot. Saini came to the crease. 3 runs to win the game and breach Australia's beloved fortress.

Pant on strike and Hazelwood to bowl the last ball of the over. He bowled a low full toss and played it straight down the track. It crossed the midfielder and went straight to the boundary. **It's India who not only won the match but the hearts of cricketing fans all over the world. They have breached Australia's pride. Yes, they have breached the Gabba, the place where Australians have never lost in the last 32 years.**

The End of an Extraordinary Fairy Tale Perhaps cricket's greatest underdog story has come to an end.

CHAPTER SEVEN

The Great Victory

19/01/2021,

The sun is setting in the Gabba, but the Indian cricket team's spirits are not. How can they after an historic win? The journey of the Indian team has been terrific in every way. The way they overcame the defeat at Adelaide and won the series is something that will always be remembered as one of the finest comebacks by an Indian team. A month ago, the Indian team was deeply buried in an incident that shocked the entire cricket world.

There were many ex-cricketers who said it's Australia who are going to have a wonderful series after their grand victory at Adelaide. There were many who estimated that India would lose the series by 0-4 to Australia. But here's something that the Indian team showed them all in return. They won the series 2-1 with their B team.

They were buried, humiliated, burst, but they were unbent. Once upon a time, there were young rookies who were given a reason to fight, and they fought like nothing mattered to them. Those young rookies are the young players who won the series by putting up what they had and showing what they were.

With each ball passing, the tension started growing. With each over passing, the hopes have been rising for the

Indian team. Rishabh Pant's innings will be remembered for a long time in cricketing history. The intent he showed and the hard work he's done will always be remembered. The innings for Pujara was so good that it had everything in it. The innings showed how determined he is. He took blows over his head, shoulders, and hands, nearly breaking his fingers, but he never gave up. The innings from Gill showed how class he is. The way he batted against the world class bowlers, mainly taking on Starc is amazing.

Sundar's assistance to Pant while chasing demonstrated how effective he was at the bottom of the order. The runs he made might be small, but they are the valuable runs that made the partnership strong and took it very close to history.

The news that India won at The Gabba is something that the Australians could not digest. But they are outclassed by an Indian B team. It's been a roller coaster ride for the Indian team. They defined the odds at every level they faced. This series had everything in it. There were heroes who showed up every time the Indian team needed them. There were players who gave everything they had.

Wishes have been sent to the Indian team from all over the world. The appreciation has been coming from all over the world. They know they have seen something that history has not witnessed. They know that this win would be a historical moment in cricket history.

The way Rahane led the Indian team after the Adelaide defeat is inspiring and motivating. The way he took decisions at every level made everyone think. The way he led the Indians in the last test is exceptional. But it's not just the captain who gave everything; it's the whole team effort that made them achieve this.

Last but not least, the series demonstrated how we can recover from the agony of defeat to the sweetness of victory. Never give up after a failure because we never know how awesome our comeback might be.

• 25 •